Contents

CAMBRIDGE UNIVERSITY PRESS

Cambridge University Press
Cambridge, New York, Melbourne, Madrid, Cape Town, Singapore, São Paulo

Cambridge University Press
The Edinburgh Building, Cambridge CB2 8RU, UK

www.cambridge.org
Information on this title: www.cambridge.org/9780521704731

First published 2007

Printed in the United Kingdom at the University Press, Cambridge

A catalogue record for this publication is available from the British Library

ISBN: 978-0-521-70473-1 paperback

Acknowledgements

Cover
Nick Diggory, Illustration Ltd

Artwork
Shark Attack: Piers Baker
Walking Through the Forest: Nick Diggory, Illustration Ltd
Days Out poster: Infuze

Texts
'Shark Attack' by Vicki Johnson; 'Walking Through the Forest' by Paul Cookson

Layout and typesetting by eMC Design Ltd, www.emcdesign.org.uk

Shark Attack

Vicki Johnson

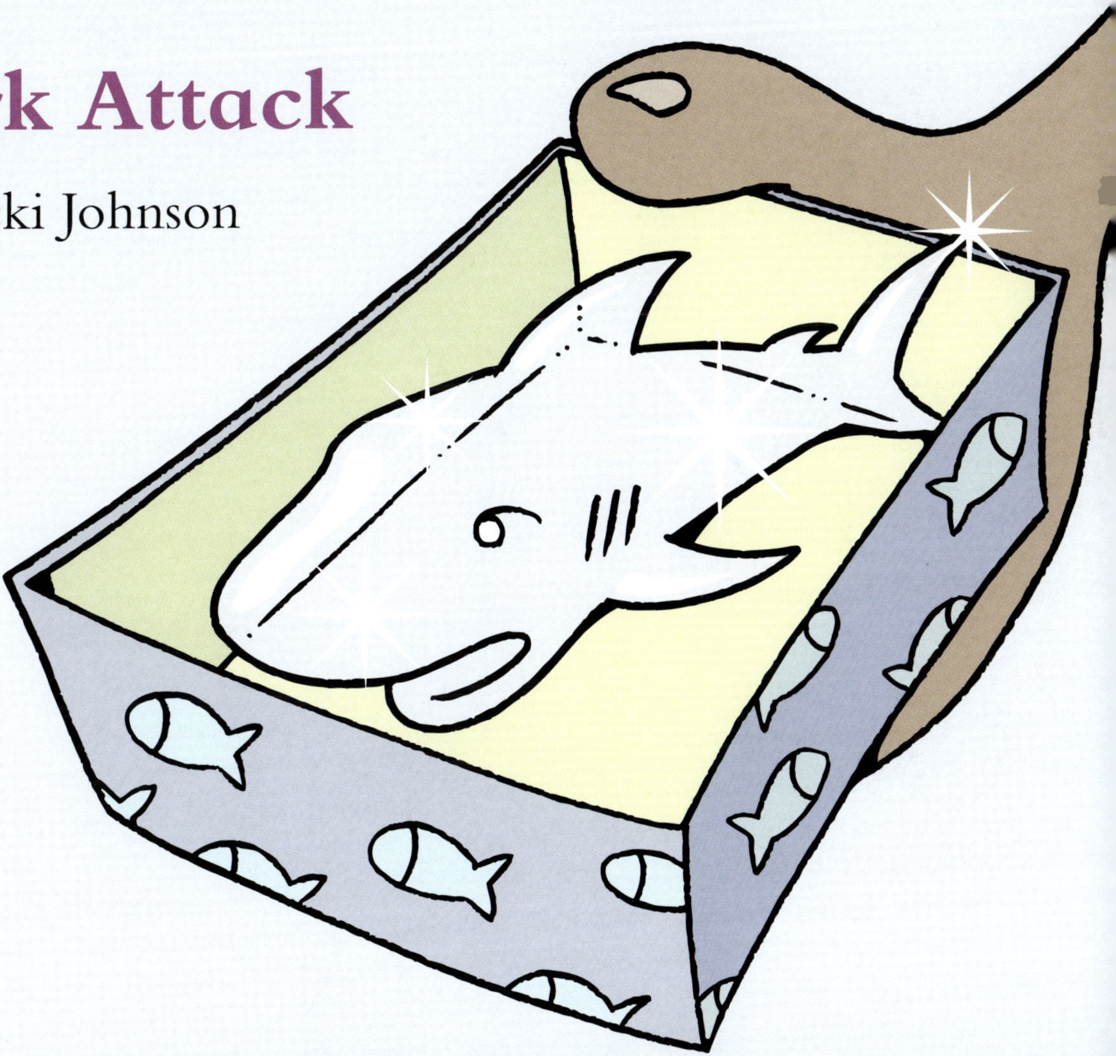

Polly Baker's birthday swimming party was at the Oasis. Polly invited her three best friends, Sophie, Anjit and Rory.

Sophie gave Polly some pink nail varnish.

"Wow!" said Polly, looking at her dad. He didn't approve of nail varnish.

Anjit's present to Polly was a friendship bracelet.

"I made it myself," she said shyly.

"Open mine now, Polly," said Rory. He handed Polly a patterned box. Inside was a glittery glass shark – the most beautiful thing Polly had ever seen.

"I chose it for you specially from Florida Sea World," said Rory.

"Right then, kids. Time to get changed," said Polly's dad. "Give me those presents, Polly. You can't take anything into the pool area apart from a towel."

Polly gave Dad her presents.
But the box Rory had given her
was empty; the precious shark
was hidden under her towel.

The noise in the Oasis reminded Polly of the school hall at dinnertime.

Anjit and Sophie jumped screaming into the deep end, but Polly and Rory sat on the side of the pool. They dipped their toes into the tepid water and stared at the twinkling shark.

"Do you like it?"
asked Rory.

"It's perfect," said Polly.

She made it zigzag towards Rory as if it was going to attack. Rory threw up his hands to protect himself and knocked the shark out of her grasp. It fell against the tiles … and smashed into a thousand pieces at the bottom of the pool.

They stared – horrified – into the water, where the pieces sparkled and shone like jewels.

"Shall we tell the lifeguards?" asked Rory anxiously.

"No way!" said Polly. "They'll kill us! Let's go and play on the slide."

They hurried down to the deep end, just as a big man waded past them and trod firmly down on to the shards of shattered shark.

"Ow! My foot!" he yelled, as he hopped up and down. "Something's cut my foot!"

Polly and Rory froze as stiff as statues.

"Please leave the pool, everyone. There's no need for alarm," shouted the lifeguard through a megaphone.

"Cor!" said Rory. "A real shark attack!"

Polly's dad appeared.

"Sorry, Polly, but the party's over. They'll have to drain the pool to find whatever hurt that man. Who knows what else is on the bottom."

Polly and Rory didn't say anything. Their hands were sticky with fear.

On Monday, everyone at school was talking about what had happened at the swimming pool.

"My mum says I'm never to go to the Oasis again," said Dexter. "She says it's dirty and dangerous."

"So does my mum," said Manu.

"They'll have to close it down," said Harry.

"They already have!" said Anjit. "There's a sign on the door which says 'closed until further notice'."

"That is so unfair!" said Sophie. "I was going to have MY party there next month."

Polly tiptoed away to find Rory.

“I didn’t mean to make the Oasis close down,” said Polly. “I was just too scared to explain how my shark ended up shattered in the pool.” They stood for a moment, scuffing their feet.

Then Polly looked at Rory and Rory looked at Polly and they both said together, "Let's tell."

Without another word, the two sorry children walked back into the school together.

"I can't say it," said Polly, "but I could write it."

Rory nodded.

This is what they wrote:

Dear Mrs Miller,

We have done something very bad. It is going to make everyone very cross with us, but if we don't tell you it will be worse. Please can you help?

Rory and Polly (Year 2)

They put the letter under the staffroom door and crept away.

For the first time since the swimming party, Polly felt as though things might – just might – eventually be all right again.

Questions

Discuss these questions with the child/children as you read through the book together.

- Why do you think Polly's dad does not approve of nail varnish? (page 6)
- When Anjit says that she made the friendship bracelet herself, why do you think she says it shyly? (page 7)
- Which of Polly's presents would you most like to be given – the nail varnish, the friendship bracelet or the shark? Why? (page 8)
- Why do you think Polly hides the shark and takes it into the swimming pool? (page 10)
- Why do you think the noise inside the Oasis reminds Polly of the school hall at dinnertime? How do you think the noise in the two places would be similar? (page 11)
- Why is the shark described as *twinkling*? What makes it twinkle? (page 11)
- Why doesn't Polly want to tell the lifeguard about the broken shark? What does she mean by *They'll kill us!*? (page 13)

- What does Rory mean by *A real shark attack*? (page 15)
- Why does the lifeguard ask everyone to leave the pool? (page 15)
- Polly's and Rory's hands are *sticky with fear*. Why do you think being frightened makes their hands sticky? (page 16)
- Why might the Oasis have to close down? (page 18)
- When Sophie talks about the party she was supposed to have at the Oasis, why does Polly tiptoe away? (page 19)
- Why do you think Rory and Polly decide to tell about the shark? (page 21)
- Why do you think it is easier for Polly to write about what happened with the shark, rather than talk to someone about it? (page 22)
- Why do Rory and Polly think people will be cross with them? (page 23)
- Why do Rory and Polly think *it will be worse* if they don't tell Mrs Miller what they have done? (page 23)
- What makes Polly think that things might be *all right again*? What does she mean by 'all right'? (page 24)

Days Out

A poem and a poster about a trip to the forest

Walking Through the Forest

Walking through the forest
Daddy and me
Things to hear
Things to see

Walking through the forest
Mummy as well
Things to touch
Things to smell

Birds in the branches
Chitta-chatta-cheep

Long, long grass
Swish-a-swish-shweep

Leaves a-crunching
Scrinch – scrunch

Branches swaying
Left – right

Walking, walking, walking
through the forest

Walking, walking, walking
through the forest

Sticky mud oozing
Squilch – squolch

Tiny twigs twitching
Crick-a-crack-snap

Woodpecker hammering
Tock-a-tock-tock

Flowers blooming
Sniff – aah

Walking through the forest
Daddy and me
Things to hear
Things to see

Walking through the forest
Mummy as well
Things to touch
Things to smell

Paul Cookson

Fancy a fun day out at half-term?
COME TO LITTLEVALE WOOD!
Tickets only £3 !!
Go deer-spotting with Safari Sam. You might even see a newborn fawn!
Walk the woodland paths and play Hide and Seek among the 500-year-old trees!
Saturday May 27th, 10am - 2pm
OPEN TO THE PUBLIC FOR ONE DAY ONLY!
500
Hunt for minibeasts! There's a prize for the scariest bug found.
Enjoy delicious home-baked cakes at the Warden's Lodge.
See the newly-hatched frogs in Frog Hollow Pond!
Spot woodpeckers and squirrels on our Little Explorers' Nature Trail!
All money will help protect woodland all over the country.

Questions

Discuss these questions with the child/children as you read through the book together.

- What is a forest called if it is in a very hot, rainy part of the world? (page 29)
- What makes the branches sway left and right? (page 31)
- Why do woodpeckers hammer at trees? (page 33)
- At what time of year do you think the people in the poem are taking their walk? Why do you think that? (page 33)
- How do you think the people are feeling as they walk through the forest? What makes you think that? (page 35)

- What is a fawn? (page 37)
- What types of minibeast do you think you might find at Littlevale Wood? (page 37)
- You can spot woodpeckers and squirrels on the Nature Trail. What other kinds of animal do you think you might find in Littlevale Wood? (page 37)